# Growing Up
# My Period

## Marissa E. Bruce
### Illustrated by Uli Ilina

*Growing Up My Period*

Copyright @ 2022
Marissa E. Bruce

Illustrated by Uli Ilina

YGTMedia Co. Press Trade Paperback Edition

Published in Canada, for Global Distribution by YGTMedia Co.

www.ygtmedia.co/publishing

SKU 978-1-998754-05-2

Printed in North America

# Growing Up
## My Period

I told a trusted grown-up, and they said I started my period. This means I am growing up.

# Symptoms

Sometimes I feel a little sick while I have my period. But it's okay because it won't last long.

## Backache

## Headache

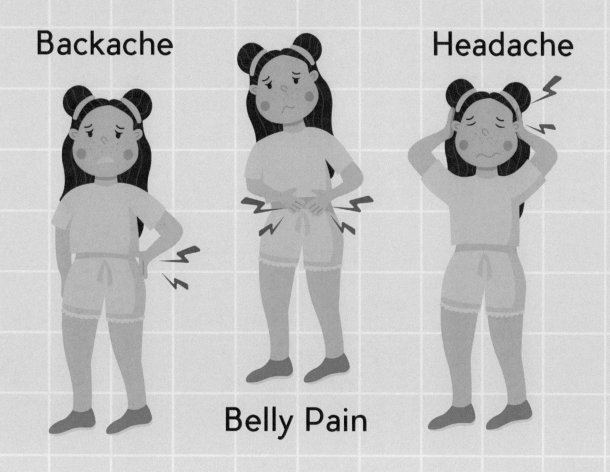

## Belly Pain

I don't feel embarrassed because this happens to all girls, but I do need to know what to do. My teacher gave me a pad and showed me what to do. Now let me show you how to use a pad, so you can be proud of your period, just like me.

# Remove sanitary pad

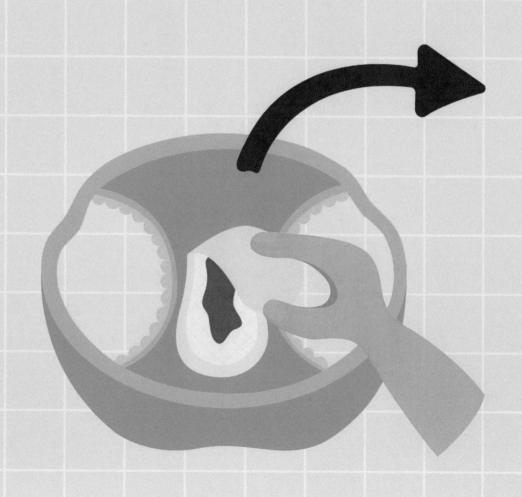

5

# Roll up
# sanitary pad

# Throw away sanitary pad

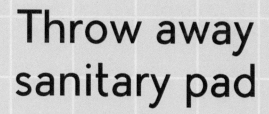

# Open new sanitary pad

# Put sanitary pad in underwear

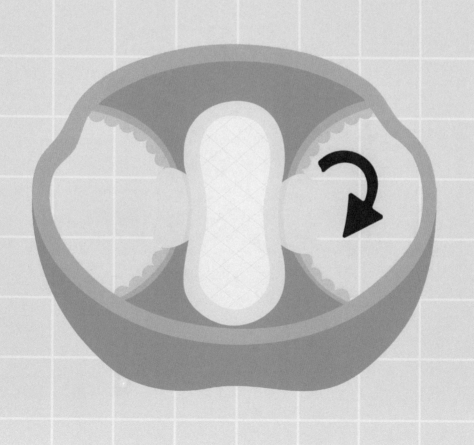

Take paper
off wings

# Stick wings under

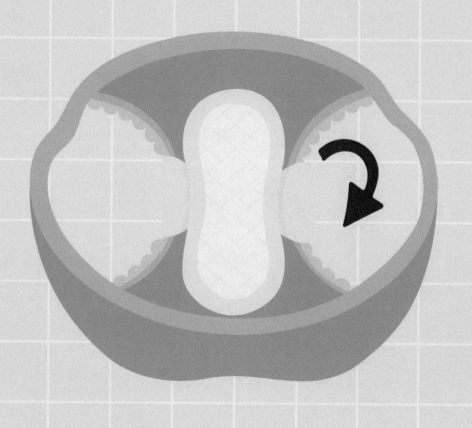

Throw out
all garbage

Wipe

# Flush

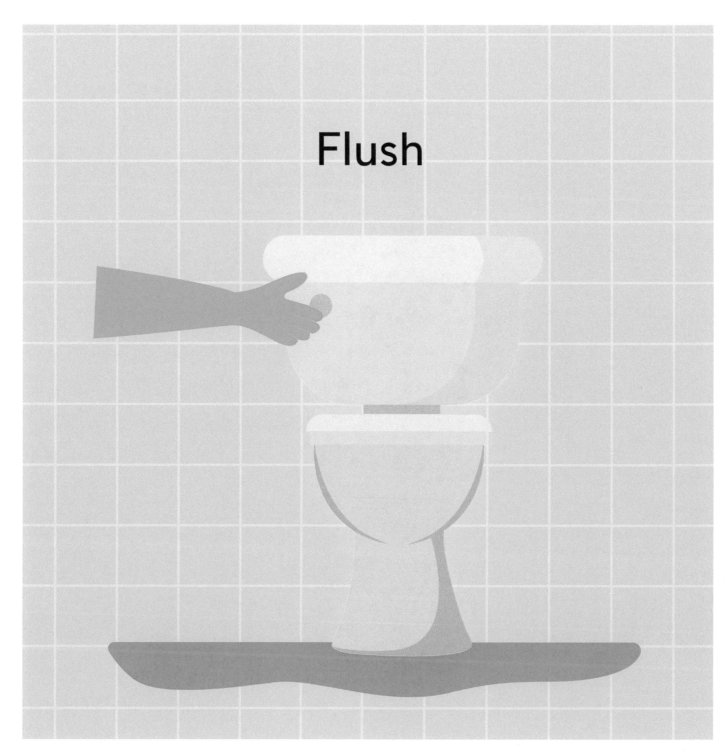

# Wash hands

# You did it!

Now that you know what to do
when you have your period,
you can be proud of growing up
just like me! If you have questions,
you can ask a trusted grown-up.

# Changing my pad

# Growing Up
## My Period

YGTMEDIA CO PUBLISHING
YGTMEDIA.CO/PUBLISHING PRINTED IN NORTH AMERICA

Made in United States
Orlando, FL
21 August 2023

36306476R00015